Animals should definitely <u>not</u> wear clothing.

Written by Judi Barrett and drawn by Ron Barrett

AN ALADDIN BOOK

Atheneum

For Amy and Valerie

PUBLISHED BY ATHENEUM
TEXT COPYRIGHT © 1970 BY JUDI BARRETT
DRAWINGS COPYRIGHT © 1970 BY RON BARRETT
ALL RIGHTS RESERVED
PUBLISHED SIMULTANEOUSLY IN CANADA BY
MCCLELLAND & STEWART LTD.
MANUFACTURED IN THE UNITED STATES OF AMERICA BY
CONNECTICUT PRINTERS, INC., BLOOMFIELD, CONN.
ISBN 0-689-70412-7
FIRST ALADDIN EDITION

Animals should definitely not wear clothing...

because
it would be
disastrous for
a porcupine,

because
a camel
might wear it
in the wrong
places,

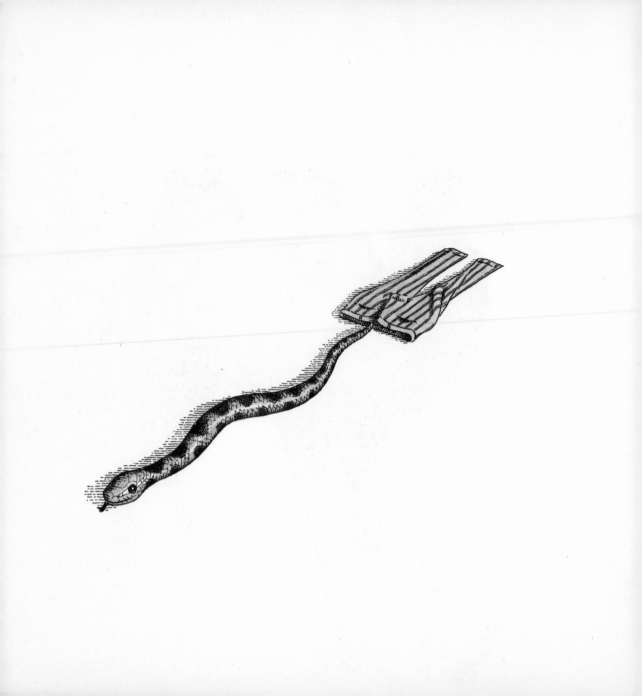

because
a snake would
lose it,

because
a mouse
could get lost
in it,

because
a sheep
might find it
terribly hot,

because
it could be
very messy
for a pig,

**because
it might
make life hard
for a hen,**

because
a kangaroo
would find it
quite
unnecessary,

because
a giraffe
might look
sort of silly,

because
a billy goat
would eat it
for lunch,

because
it would always
be wet
on a walrus,

because
a moose
could never
manage,

because
opossums
might wear it
upside down
by mistake,

and most of all, because it might be very embarrassing.

Judi Barrett divides her days between teaching art to children and writing children's books.

Ron Barrett spends his nights illustrating the books she writes, and his days as an Art Director at a New York advertising agency.

Animals should definitely <u>not</u> wear clothing is their second book. Their first one was *Old MacDonald Had An Apartment House.*

They both firmly believe that animals should definitely not wear clothing, except for an occasional dog coat on below freezing days.

This is where they draw the line.